What's the MATTER with the Three Little Pigs?

The Fairy-Tale Physics of Matter

by Thomas Kingsley Troupe

illustrated by Jomike Tejido

PICTURE WINDOW BOOKS
a capstone imprint

Once upon a time, there was a family of pigs. A huge family. A family that was outgrowing its house.

"I'm sorry, you three, but you're old enough to be on your own now," Mama Pig said. "I need the room."

Steve, Hector, and Alice were sad. But they knew Mama was right. It was time for them to go.

Steve packed his teddy bear. Alice grabbed a few books. Hector filled his suitcase with mud. Alice shook her head at her little brother.

"What's the matter?" Hector asked. "Mud is magic."

"No, mud is matter," Alice said. "It's basic physics."

"Huh?" Hector said.

No pig knew more about science than Alice. She loved reading about how things worked. "Matter is the stuff that's all around us," she explained. "Everything in the world is matter: you, me, mud, this house, that wolf on TV . . ."

A photo of a wolf had popped up on the TV screen. The reporter said the police were looking for him. B.B. Wulf had scared a little girl in a red riding hood. He was dangerous and still on the loose.

Before the three pigs left, they looked at ads in the newspaper.

"We each need to find a house that will keep us safe from the wolf," Steve said. "Something solid."

"Solid?" Hector said. "What does that mean?"

"Well, Hector," Alice said, "there are three basic states of matter." She pointed to a tree in the yard. "That tree is a *solid* form of matter. Solids are the strongest. They hold their shape. The pond water over there is a *liquid* form of matter."

"What's the third form?" Hector asked.

"Gas," Alice said. "The air around us is a gas called oxygen. Gases are almost always invisible."

Hector giggled over the word "gas" and looked at the house ads again. He circled his favorite. Steve and Alice each circled their favorite too. After hugging Mama, the three pigs headed out into the world.

The next day, Steve stood proudly at his new house. A houseboat. It floated near the middle of Lake Donut. Steve liked how the lake was shaped like a donut. But he *didn't* like that there was something hairy creeping along the shore.

"Little pig, little pig, in the middle of the lake," the creature said, "I'm going to eat you like a birthday cake!"

It was B.B. Wulf!

"You can't get here unless you swimmy, swim, swim!" Steve shouted back. "And you don't look like a great swimmer."

"Then I'll wait, and I'll howl, until the snow begins to fall," the wolf replied.

Steve shook his head. "That was a really awful rhyme," he said.

The wolf shrugged and said, "I agree, it wasn't a winner, my soon-to-be pork-chop dinner."

The snow fell hard. Really hard. It was one of the biggest, coldest snowstorms ever. Steve watched as the water in Lake Donut changed.

"Oh, now I'm oinked," Steve said. "I forgot that matter can change states."

"I'm going to eat you with butter and rice," the wolf called, "as soon as the lake water turns to ice!"

Steve grunted in horror as the water froze. The liquid had become a solid! B.B. Wulf started skating across the frozen lake.

"I've got to get out of here!" Steve said.

"Little pig, little pig, where are you going?" B.B. Wulf called. "You won't get far, now that it's snowing!"

"Your rhymes stink!" Steve shouted, scrambling off into the night to find Hector.

Some time later, Steve found Hector's house. It was made entirely of ice. Steve knocked hard on the front door until Hector opened it.

"Hi, Steve," Hector said.

"No time for that, bro," Steve said, pushing aside his brother. "That wolf is hot on my curly tail!"

HECTOR'S HOUSE

Hector closed the door and locked it. "Don't worry," he said. "We're safe in here. The walls are made of solid ice. Come on, let's skate!"

He tossed Steve a pair of skates, and the two skated around Hector's living room. They sang songs and forgot all about B.B. Wulf.

Until a knock came at the door.

Hector looked through the peephole.

"Oh, mud. It's that Wulf guy," he said.

"You can't escape me one way or another," B.B. Wulf called. "Now I'll eat you *and* your piggy brother!"

"You'll never get in. We're surrounded by icy, ice, ice!" Steve shouted.

The wolf smiled, took out his cell phone, and tapped a few times.

"Oh, that's fine. You can stop your yipping," B.B. Wulf said. "I've just placed an order with next-day shipping."

Steve and Hector couldn't imagine what that awful wolf was up to.

Very early the next morning, a delivery truck arrived. And what did B.B. Wulf get? A flamethrower! He squeezed the trigger. Fire shot out.

"Little pigs, little pigs, I don't mean to boast," he began. "But this is sure to be the best-ever pig roast."

Steve and Hector watched as the walls of Hector's house turned from a solid to a liquid.

"The fire is changing the state of the matter!" Steve shouted. "Your ice house is turning into water!"

"Let's go!" Hector said.

The pigs ran out the back door and hid behind some bushes.

The wind blew hard and cold. It nipped at Steve and Hector as they watched B.B. Wulf melt the house to the ground.

The wolf sniffed the air. He chuckled. "The ice house is melted," he said. "No dinner was inside. But I can smell you're near, pigs! You cannot hide!"

B.B. Wulf started creeping toward the bushes. He crept closer and closer. Just before he reached Steve and Hector, he took a step and . . . fell onto his furry bottom.

"Nice!" Steve said. "A little patch of water re-froze and changed back to ice!"

"Matter can change back to its old state?" Hector asked.

"Sometimes, yes, and sometimes, no," Steve said. "It depends on the matter."

Before the wolf could get up, the two brothers ran off to find their sister.

Alice's cabin was made of stone, with log posts out front. The brothers pounded on the heavy door.

"Hey, guys!" Alice said. "Come in. I'm about to make some tea."

Steve and Hector hurried inside and told Alice their stories.

"He won't get in here," Alice said. "This place is made of solid stone. And the wood won't melt like ice."

The teapot blew its whistle. Little puffs of steam escaped through the spout.

Hector pointed at the stove. "Your water's whistling," he said.

"Matter is changing!" Alice said. "The water inside the teapot changes to a gas, or evaporates, when it's heated. Some of it escapes through the hole. That's what makes the whistle blow."

Steve peered out the window.

"We might need to make an escape too," he said.

B.B. Wulf was back.

"Little pigs, little pigs, when will you learn?" the wolf sang. "Ice can melt, and wood can burn!"

The wolf shot fire from his flamethrower, and the wood on Alice's cabin started to burn.

"Don't worry, boys," Alice said. "The state of the wood is changing, but fire can't burn stone."

Steve opened the window and yelled, "Nice try, dog breath! We're all safe in here from your teethy, teeth, teeth!"

Once the wood was burned up, B.B. Wulf tossed aside his flamethrower and disappeared into the woods.

"Is he gone?" Hector asked.

"I hope so," Steve said.

Suddenly, a rumble shook the house. Out of the woods rolled a giant crane with a wrecking ball. B.B. Wulf sat in the driver's seat.

"I'm going to make these quiet woods louder, as I knock your little piggy house down to powder!" he shouted.

The wolf wiggled the crane's controls. The big arm swung back, then forward. The wrecking ball smashed into the side of Alice's cabin with a **BOOM!**

"Oh no!" Alice cried.

"I thought this house was solid," Hector said.

"It is," Steve said. "The wolf's not changing the state of Alice's house. He's changing the shape."

"The rock pieces are still solids," Alice said. "But they won't keep us safe anymore."

So the three pigs ran as fast they could into the woods.

Soon they came upon a small roadside stand selling hot-air balloon rides. It was the perfect getaway. They bought their tickets, hopped in, and quickly rose into the sky. Hector looked at the big balloon above them.

"Alice, is that a gas in there?" he asked.

"Yes," Alice said. "It's called helium. Gases expand to fill the container they're in. The balloon above us is a kind of container."

"Unlike solids," Steve added, "gases don't have their own definite shape. They take the shape of whatever container they're in."

"That's all very cool," Hector said. "But look! There's another balloon full of gas heading our way!"

Yep. It was B.B. Wulf.

"Little pigs, little pigs, high up in the sky," he called, "don't you three know that pigs can't fly?"

Steve frowned. "I really don't like this guy," he said.

"We need to be lighter so we can go up higher," Alice said. "Quick, throw some weights overboard."

The pigs untied the basket's weights. Even so, the wolf got closer. Steve pointed at Hector's suitcase.

"Sorry, Hector," Steve said. "Your suitcase has to go."

"But my mud reminds me of home," Hector said. He opened up his luggage to show his brother. But the squishy mud had hardened into a block.

"The mud changed states," Alice said. "It's a solid now!"

"Oh," Hector said. "Then never mind."

And without warning, Hector tossed the heavy block of dried mud over the side of the basket. The chunk landed on the wolf's balloon.

POP! HISSSSSSSS!

"Nice shot, bro!" Steve shouted.

The pigs watched as the balloon lost its gas. It zipped back and forth across the sky, sending B.B. Wulf and his horrible rhymes far, far away.

"Where are we going to live now?" Hector asked.

"For you, Hector, some place with mud, I suppose," Alice said. "But with that wolf gone, does it MATTER where we go?"

Glossary

evaporate—to change from a liquid to a gas

expand—to grow larger

freeze—to change from a liquid to a solid because of cold

gas—a form of matter that is not solid or liquid; it can move about freely and does not have a definite shape

liquid—matter that is wet and can be poured, such as water

matter—anything that has mass and takes up space

physics—the science that deals with matter and energy; physics includes the study of light, heat, sound, electricity, motion, and force

solid—a substance that holds its shape

state—a form a substance takes, such as a solid, liquid, or gas

Critical Thinking Questions

1. Look at the illustration on page 21 and find examples of all three basic states of matter: solid, liquid, and gas.

2. Give an example from the story of a solid turning into a liquid. What made the solid change states?

3. Describe how the story would've been different if there hadn't been a terrible snowstorm.

Read More

Housel, Debra J. *The Nature of Matter.* Physical Science. Huntington Beach, Calif.: Teacher Created Materials, 2015.

Rompella, Natalie. *Experiments in Material and Matter with Toys and Everyday Stuff.* Fun Science. North Mankato, Minn.: Capstone Press, a Capstone imprint, 2016.

Troupe, Thomas Kingsley. *Are Bowling Balls Bullies?: Learning About Forces and Motion with the Garbage Gang.* The Garbage Gang's Super Science Questions. North Mankato, Minn.: Picture Window Books, a Capstone imprint, 2016.

Internet Sites

Use FactHound to find Internet sites related to this book.

Visit *www.facthound.com*

Just type in 9781515828969 and go.

Look for all the books in the series!

Index

Special thanks to our adviser, Darsa Donelan, Professor of Physics,
Gustavus Adolphus College, Saint Peter, Minnesota, for her expertise.

Editor: Jill Kalz
Designer: Lori Bye
Premedia Specialist: Tori Abraham
The illustrations in this book were created digitally.

Picture Window Books
1710 Roe Crest Drive
North Mankato, MN 56003
www.mycapstone.com

Library of Congress Cataloging-in-Publication data is available on the Library of Congress website.
ISBN 978-1-5158-2896-9 (library binding)
ISBN 978-1-5158-2900-3 (paperback)
ISBN 978-1-5158-2904-1 (eBook PDF)

Summary: What's the matter with the three little pigs? They're being tormented by a hungry wolf, that's what!
And no matter what kind of matter they use to build their homes, it doesn't matter. The STEM-savvy, rhyme-
loving wolf in this fractured fairy tale always seems to spoil the day.

Printed in the United States   5273